Flicker Flash

To Mom and Dad
Jim, Heather, and Aimee
family and friends
especially Shirley, Jane, Pat, and Mona—
thank you for lighting my way
—J. B. G.

To my parents
Thank you for encouraging me to follow my star.
—N. D.

Text copyright © 1999 by Joan Bransfield Graham
Illustrations copyright © 1999 by Nancy Davis

www.houghtonmifflinbooks.com

Library of Congress Cataloging-in-Publication Data

Graham, Joan Bransfield.
Flicker flash / Joan Bransfield Graham ; illustrated by Nancy Davis.
p. cm.
Summary: A collection of poems celebrating light in its various forms, from candles and
lamps to lightning and fireflies.
RNF ISBN 0-395-90501-X   PAP ISBN 0-618-31102-5
1. Light — Juvenile poetry. 2. Children's poetry, American. [1. Light — Poetry. 2. American
poetry.] I. Davis, Nancy, 1949–   ill. II. Title.
PS3557.R213F55   1999
811'.54 — dc21   98-12956 CIP AC

Manufactured in China
LEO 20 19 18 17 16
4500351738

Flicker Flash

poems by Joan Bransfield Graham

illustrated by Nancy Davis

Light

Light,
light,
stretch
my sight,
bend back
c o r n e r s
of the night.
Flicker, flash,
near and far,
turn on lamps,
& sprinkle stars.
One small flame,
a tiny spark . . .
or wide as day,
you scatter dark.

Sun

"From 93,000,000 miles away I bring you this dynamite, ring-a-ding day. I'll shout in your window and bounce near your head to solar power you out of your bed!"

Candle

CANDLE

You
promise quick,
exotic light,
a dancing
vision of
the night,
you give
the room
a painted
face that
blinks and
winks and
helps erase
the feeling
of the empty
black that's
slyly creeping
up my back.

Days and Years

earth   s u m m e r f
is spinning
toward the light,
first it's day,
and then it's
night

a r o u n d   t h e   s u n

Firefly

Firefly, flit high then low do you know what makes you glow?

Crescent Moon

new

grin

moon

night

sliver

the

thin

see

nice to

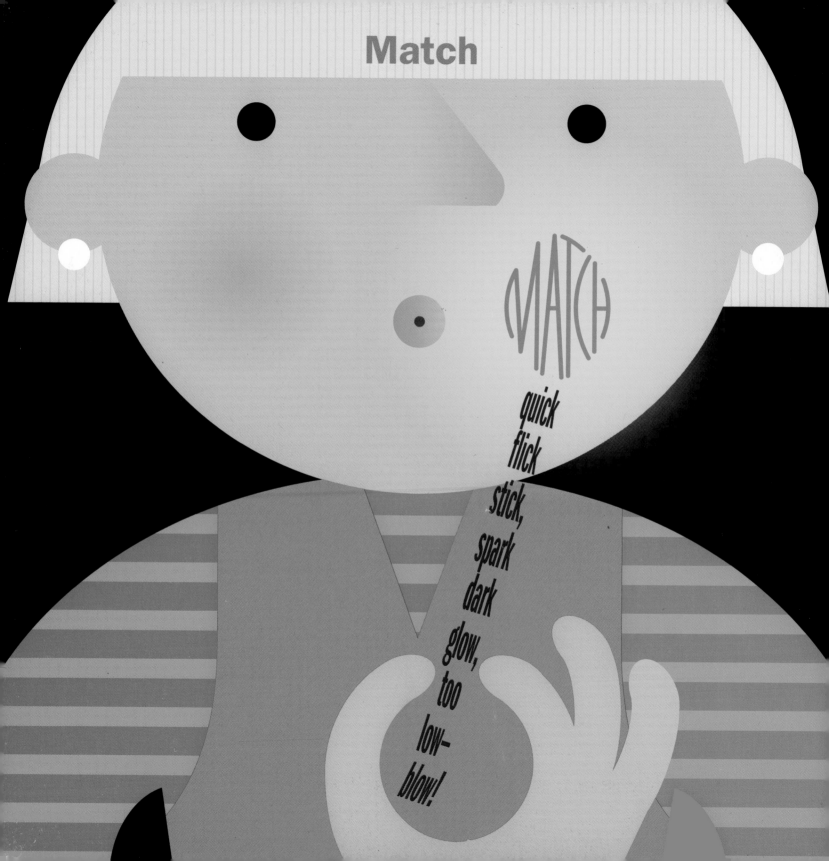

Birthday Candles

Happy Day Happy Year

Like shooting stars that blaze the dark, you flame — then disappear. But when I look, I see your light in faces, circled near.

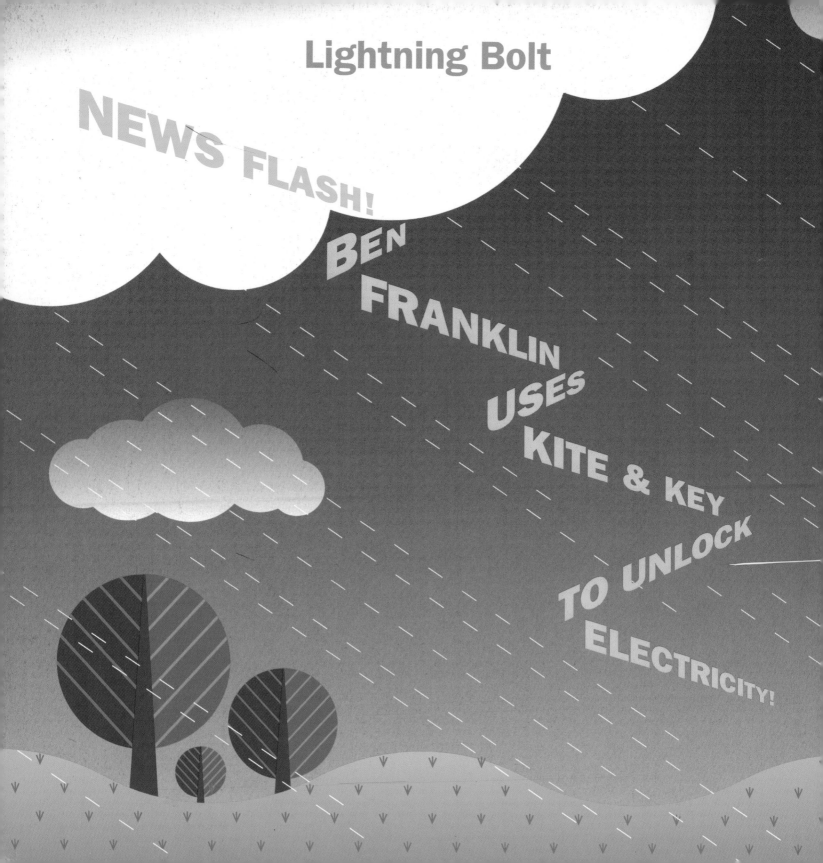

Light Bulb

Thomas
Edison didn't
hesitate to let
ideas incubate, and
try again, if they
weren't right. One
day to his intense
delight, he squeezed
his thoughts
into a bulb
and then
turned
on the
light
light
light
!!!

Stars

in
space

star
mail

can
seem

quite
slow

this card
was sent

Full Moon

like
a *MIRROR*,
far away, moon
REFLECTS the
flames of day, in
a *SILVER* kind
of way

ago

light
years

GIVE-IT-
ALL-

YOU'VE-GOT
LIGHT

NOW

LIGHT

A BOW LIGHT

a luminous square box brings light through wires and air, shows superheroes save the world while I'm just s i t t i n g there

Refrigerator Light

Open the door.

By the light in the refrigerator, I can plainly see that the Brussels sprouts are meant for Y O U . . . the chocolate cake's for ME.

Lighthouse

LIG

Oh, Captain of the midnight sky, you stretch your arms and flash your eye across the waves and churning foam to steer me, guide me, safely HOME.

LIGHT HOUSE

FLASH

**OPEN THE SHUTTER
SUNLIGHT WILL SPILL
ONTO MY FILM
TO MAKE TIME
STAND STILL**

**Warm
as a hen,
this toasty
trick will turn
an egg into
a chick!**

PEEP
PEEP

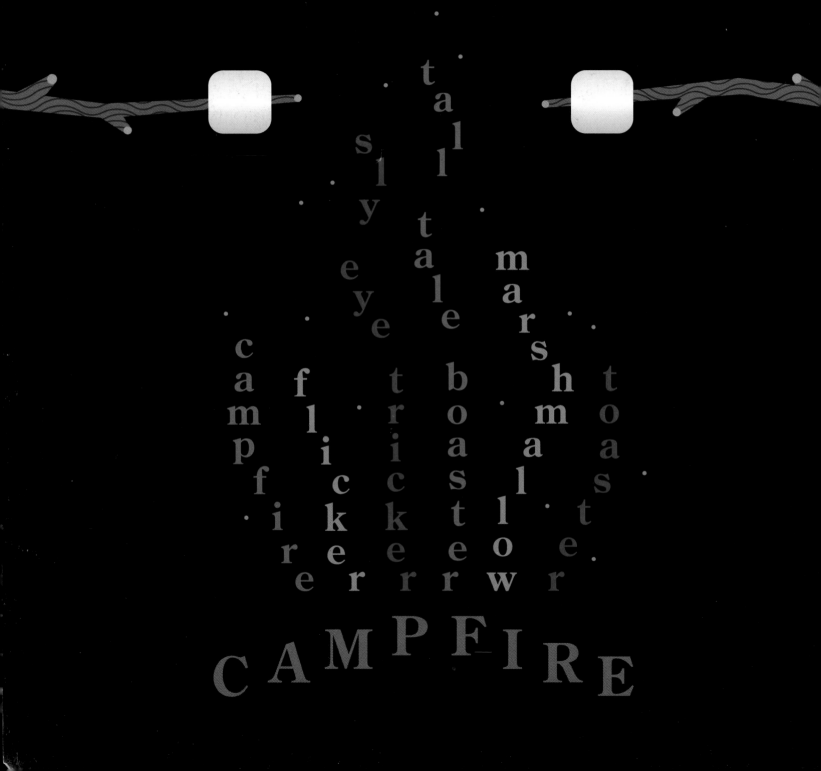

CAMPFIRE

Flashlight

click
one flick
I am the SUN,
I chase the shadows
one by one, growing scary,
jagged, tall – with brilliant beams
I'll MELT them ALL!

shooting up high, scattering across the sky petals?

Lamp

soft gold
lamp-shine makes
this book *all mine*, in
this welcome curve of light,
nestled in the lap of night

L
A
M
P
L A M P